Each
Unkept
Secret

Each Unkept Secret

Donna Prinzmetal

MoonPath Press

Poetry
ISBN 978-1-936657-85-8

Cover art: I.H. Prinzmetal, *Holmby Park*
Photographed by Aaron Wessling
of Portland Art Documentation
https://www.portlandartdocumentation.com/

Author photo: Stephen Kirsch

Book design: Tonya Namura, using
Garamond Premier Pro (text) and Sofia Pro (display).

MoonPath Press, an imprint of Concrete Wolf Poetry Series,
is dedicated to publishing the finest poets living in
the U.S. Pacific Northwest.

MoonPath Press
c/o Concrete Wolf
PO Box 2220
Newport, OR 97365-0163

MoonPathPress@gmail.com

http://MoonPathPress.com

For the mothers

Table of Contents

Each
Unkept
Secret

I

There's No Going Back Now

At the Mahogany Table

My mother fingers the silver bell,
her pale skin marked with brown spots.
My hand looks small next to hers.
Everyone is talking at once.
On my plate, the pink roast beef
drowns in gravy. A half-eaten popover
has melted the round scoop of butter.

Mother smells of Replique and cigarettes.
I can't stop looking at the yellow and brown cityscape—
my father's painting—on the wall,
tall geometric shapes, its oil smell.

The dining room echoes with voices,
645 Comstock in spring, the end of another school year,
almost. My sister Jan laughs too loud.
Debbie hasn't changed her name yet.
Dad is at the other end, his voice so deep
it rumbles under my chair. "You need to pay attention
to the details," he says. They are talking
about Debbie's valedictorian speech. It's 1967.

My white cardigan with the tiny fake pearl buttons
is too warm. I'm afraid I'll get butter on the sleeves
so I take it off. My hair is short and still gold,
but it's growing out and tickles my ears.

I am so used to this cacophony, everyone talking at once.
When a new voice, higher than I expect
rises with a kind of ping, I feel it in the back of my throat.
"What about starting with a list? All those science projects,"
I say, out loud, it seems. I don't even believe it's me.
I am thinking of ideas for her speech, but nobody
pays attention, except my oldest sister, Karen.

Her brown eyes meet my blue ones.
"Wait," she says in a voice of rare authority,
"Donna said something."
She emphasizes my name, though she couldn't
have heard exactly what I said.
There is a break in the clink of silver knives on white Wedgewood,
and the voices, the voices have all stopped.

There could be a floodlight bathing me
in a waterfall of white. I feel laid bare, naked, cold.
Gooseflesh rises on my arms
as everyone begins to clap. It is the first time
I have spoken at the dinner table

ever. I am eleven years old.
I want to hide in the kitchen
at the little kid's table.
I want to pick up the gravy boat
and dive into it.

Everyone is looking at me.
I slip down in the stiff-backed dining room chair.
My blue shift clings to my sticky thighs.

I have spoken. They know I can speak.
There's no going back now.

Nomenclature

My mother dies twenty-nine years after my father.

There has never been a word for this. *Orphan* won't cut it,
this split-open jagged wound that can't be closed.

It's what we want, isn't it, to be known,
to be labeled for the damaged goods that we are?

Whatever life you have led, and whatever lens
you have looked through, you know this.

Remember feeling for the light switch on the wall
even in a blackout, imagining some ordinary glitch

has landed you in this immaculate dark?
You know what it's like—

the laundered myths that should explain the beast
hovering in the corner of that room, fangs bared,

harbinger of the campfire becoming wildfire.
There should be a word for that.

If only I could find the right syntax
for grieving, the right vocabulary.

I want to drink the nectar of words,
feel the carnal caress, the manna,

the exact syllables shaping in my mouth.
Weepingness should be a word.

Who couldn't get behind weepingness?
And we, the proud misfits

could move to that country
where aloneness is commonplace as shadows.

Inheritance

From my mother, I inherited a dwarfed pinky toe,
one tiny white spot on my skin, wide hips.

From my father, his love for the Impressionists,
his craving for books.

From the poets, in spite of all efforts to the contrary,
I inherited a love of dead things:

the threadbare gold skeletons of last year's tomatillos,
the artichoke flowers that turn to dust

when I try to hold them.
And once, in Kelly Park,

the translucent white ghosts of a mother and daughter
swinging their legs from the branch of an old oak,

that diaphanous light,
their unendurable beauty.

Lens

I am not born yet, not even anticipated.
Before the white house on Comstock Avenue,
up the sprawling driveway,
the sweet lavender wisteria, the blacktop
where we tried to fry an egg.

There is a party, elegant summer dresses.
She laughs and covers the excruciating gap
between her front teeth.
He looks handsome in a dark suit.
She is there with the heart surgeon,
his brother, before he went crazy.
They look at each other across the lighted patio;
he asks his brother permission to dance with her
in the saucy jazz-spiked evening,
glass of bruised moonlight.
She is still thin. Her hair
falls in delicate wisps.

She dances with Errol Flynn (yes, really)
but all she will talk about the next day
is my father, a relief
from her cold mother,
the crevasse of childhood
she clambers to escape.
Her bright eyes, winking back at Orion.
She is twenty-two; he is thirty-six.
She has such hopes.

And all these years later, if Forgiveness is a country,
can I speak its language? Is it a place
like Chicago or the French Riviera?
I visit it frequently, as I visit her persimmon tree
and the Chinese elm

in front of the house on Comstock,
all the years telescoped together.

I imagine the two of them
in that first dance.
I am already arriving, even then.

The Photograph

I want to hide in those folds of my mother's white shift
before she was my mother.

The brocade around her neck is as delicate as she was then.
In the photograph, she has the bright eyes

of a kingfisher. The sepia tone
doesn't show their ocean color

but you can still see the shine. Her lips are parted
and I cannot see her teeth though I know

they were tiny like mine, with a space
that made her cover her mouth when she laughed,

until Father took her to a dentist
three weeks after their wedding, and had them capped.

I can almost see her small hand struggle
to stretch an octave.

She looks twelve or thirteen next to the thin limbs
of a pear tree. My father, an older man

she thought would take care of her, take her
away from her mother,

the mother who held her love like a bright pear,
red, on a branch out of reach.

White Lies

for my mother

You didn't dance with Errol Flynn.

You never bought a sheep farm in Southern Oregon.

You never swallowed a whole bottle of aspirin
and said, "I'm sorry I'm sorry I'm sorry"
flat, from the hospital gurney.

You didn't sit on the ledge of my bed, teary
to tell me Martin Luther King had died.

You never snuck cigarettes like a five-year-old;
we never had to search your purse
and tear apart the ones we found.

In a manic frenzy, you never went wild
with a charge card buying shoes and clothes
that never fit any of us.

You never had shock treatments.

I never had to remind you where you were
or who I was.

You never had lovers
and Father never knew about them.

You never called me at school, on a Thursday in March
to say he had died.

You never lumbered out, on your bad legs, from your bed
in the dark, away from the nurse, to make it to a storage room
for a can of sardines.

It didn't take three of us to pull you up.

You never read to me
Edna St. Vincent Millay's "Ballad of the Harp Weaver."

You didn't know the name of every orchid,
even when people's names began to elude you.

You didn't love your roses, especially the Double Delights.

You didn't love me.

We didn't listen to Rachmaninoff's Concerto #3
or your labored breathing. I wasn't holding
your thick warm hand while the new day gathered
at the hospital window.

We didn't scatter your ashes in that rose garden.

I never think about you.

I don't think about you every day.

Origins

I am from a long line of grumbling stomachs,
the hearty Russian stock of borscht
and potatoes, the rancid melting pot
of shapeless black dresses, woven breads,
hanging bosoms, and from the French Alps,
every haunted song of cabbage,
yeasty mornings.

Mother learned the ancient art of making fudge
from her mother, from whom she also inherited
several missing teeth. In a dirty apron,
stirring and tasting and blotting and burning,
a blurb of boiling chocolate dropped
in a cup of cold water, testing to see
if the fudge had cooked long enough,
cracked stubby fingers that molded the little drip of goo.
"Not quite," she whispered, more to herself than to me.

Who would bother shaping butter
to "the size of an egg"? Trying to figure out
what a ten-cent bottle of cream might be?
She was a sloppy cook, a slurping and dirty cook.
The red leather benches, the wallpaper
peeling at the edges in the hot afternoon kitchen,
the gas stove dribbled with gravies or pasta sauce,
happy splatter of bacon grease.

She continued her work with the wooden spoon
until she stopped being able to cook for herself,
sagged beneath the weight of her excesses.
I have inherited her love of butter, chocolate, rich sauces.
I am pondering fudge tonight, not this great blue heron
in front of me now, searching for dinner,
as water laps up and tickles her tail feathers,

but my own brief forage
into a sunlit kitchen far from here.

My Father's Painting

Once, long ago, my father painted the yellow hills
in his green velour sweatshirt, spattered with color.
The Santa Monica Mountains: that distant chaparral
with its yellow-eyed grass and monkey flower,
Indian paintbrush and fire poppy. On the canvas,
the red and gold looked like fire.

A robin darts in and out of shadows. The open wound
of the weeping cherry is filled with dirt.
Where the enormous oak once stood, a patch
of lonely grass. On crisp cold days
I am less aware of what I miss.

My father's voice was base-drum deep,
and his hair, still dark but thin,
strands of grass on the bald hill
of his pate, shining through like something
secret on a mountain in the distance.

At night, when he couldn't sleep,
he'd walk out in slippers to his studio.
The linoleum, speckled black and white,
camouflaged the bright drops of paint when they fell,
the room rich with that odor.

My father died only two years older
than I am now, my husband's age.
A teenager, I wrote poems riddled with rhymes
and angst in that green velour shirt.

That hill painting hangs on my family room wall.
I see the sharp contours of the mountains
blazing with hot gold and rust, and above,
sunset red, angry. I hadn't noticed

the cliffs' chiseled edges, how dark
and monstrous they were,
how dangerous the sky.

Before

There was a morning
with bright September sunlight
a porch overlooking the canopy of trees
in the park. Glossy polished hardwood
and the square card table, when my father
asked for my help. Before my sister did
everything she did, before the bright
red and blue ambulance lights in the carport.
Before the glass tumbler hurled, shattered
on the wall above my head.
My dad was editing the law review,
could handle the writing
and the speeching, and all the brainy parts
but pointed to the gray scotch tape dispenser.
Before the tracks on my sister's arms
and the parties, before the bottle of aspirin
and the hospital. Before the insomnia and the Seconal
and the wet canvases in the morning,
my father patted the yellow seat next to him and said,
"Got a minute?" before my hair had lost its gold.
I was to tear out each piece of scotch tape
and put them on the paper, securing the columns
in place, before such things were done online.
My serious father smiled as I got the hang of
taping the paper where he held it, before everything
came apart, before my mother called the principal's
office where I waited and said, "I have some bad news."
Before the principal, who was a woman, lit her pipe,
before pipe smoke smelled like death,
I performed this small service for my father,
a big man who painted landscapes and taught
art students and law students and edited this
important journal. His fingers could stretch more
than an octave and he could sight read Chopin and Bach

but couldn't tear the small strips of tape
and make sure they stuck in just the right spot.
It was later, much later, that I thought maybe
he just wanted me to feel important
this one time, maybe it was his service
to me, way before I became a parent,
before I knew about sacrifice,
about survival.

What You Leave Behind

for Else Kristina Hansen, who helped raise us

The careful tending of bouquets,
small miracles of color,
all those crossword puzzles.
Your crooked fingers delicate on rose stems.

You leave behind coffee and Angel Dessert.
I wear your tan loafers that suffocate my wide feet,
so I can still hear them in the stairwell
as if you are always arriving.

Aebleskiver on New Year's morning.
Summers of wet sand in Marina Del Rey,
watching us make handprints
and sand castles.

I hear your voice in its stark unraveling.
You leave behind words,
some in Danish, your English forgotten
and out of order in your last days.

In the languid afternoon,
you leave behind a Lanz nightgown
I wore at twelve,
covered in first blood.

Macaroni and cheese
with strawberry jam,
and rain. You leave behind rain
and your love of rain.

A pink chair. Tuborg beer.
The fine china with green leaves

looks almost like the urn
holding what's left of you.

You leave me the Royal Copenhagen
figures called *The Four Pains,*
small green figures of children
in various states of distress.

None of them look like me
walking on the river of grief
chasing the last light,
what you left behind

glimmering,
sleek as a new skin
I've never worn in this life
without you.

That Door

If I could, would I go back
to that room with the big window
in the house on Comstock Avenue
looking out at that towering eucalyptus
with peeling bark I could smell
from my single bed shoved in the corner
against the white headboard
hiding a cache of troll dolls?
My sisters and I called them *Damn Dolls*
and I kept mine long after
I stopped playing with dolls.
In that headboard: all my silver dollars
and a blue paisley pencil holder
a boy had given me on my tenth birthday.

That room with a gold chain that locked
the door that led outside to the carport.
I could have gone out anytime I wanted.
They must have known, my parents—
although I wanted to—
I would never put on a strapless dress,
unchain that door and sneak out
into the night of a long-ago summer,
with no one to slink past,
walk down the driveway
and into a waiting red convertible.

My oldest sister skipped school
and ran away to look for Superman.
My parents knew I'd stay put,
sit at the tiny desk, with one red,
one yellow, and one orange drawer,
all full of poems and books.

Where would I go?
The park across the street
with its tadpole streams
and bamboo hiding places?

How I envied my sisters,
their flashy rebellion and successes,
the one with tracks on her arms
whose whole life was a secret and a lie,
the one with a steady stream of admirers,
boyfriends and parties, who still got straight A's.
What was I compared to them,
small and silent and predictable.
Only my dolls were disobedient
with their shocking pink and yellow hair.

Would I go back to that little room
with the big window
and the white shag carpet
and the closet where my cat had kittens
and the desk with the Smith Corona typewriter?
Would I unhook the gold chain
just so I could see what it was like, finally,
to run away from home?

This Is About Daughters
and What They Know

In some small child-like terror
I might never sleep again,
believe you are already gone
with eyes open, concave face,
fluorescent hospital light, favorite
piano music, and your breathing,
blessed drowning sound,
heartache of your breath,
dark waves of your breath.

Like a report after a car wreck,
the body registers its damage:
brown spots on white vitiligo skin,
pale swollen feet, arms
dimpled and picked
by yellow fingernails.
Mourning is its own language.

Mother, we are still in exile.
I review what I miss
as if it were a science
like fingerprint analysis,
or wind energy, the windmill
turning on the edge of its own ache.
How can I measure the distance
between the living and the dead?

Repast

After your long love affair with food
you had lost your appetite.
I could hardly stand it.

We both knew it wouldn't be long.
Then you came home from the hospital
finally hungry, starving even, your gift to me.

It was my birthday week.
I would have fixed anything you wanted
to see your mouth form a dark O,

your eyes crinkling with delight: tuna
and cottage cheese with lemon.
I so wanted you to eat and you did,

the first time all week. I was so glad
to fix you another portion. The air
warm for December, your hands

shook a little but you seemed grateful for
breathing, though hard, grateful for the food,
and the sun. When you finished eating,

I held your hand.

At Fourteen

It's a year after my father's death,
and my mother sleeps late.
We don't wake her.

The peeling birch bark breaks off
with a satisfying crack.
Underneath is baby-smooth skin.

Across the street in the park,
I keep company with bees as they hover
around the misshapen mess of honeysuckle.

My sandaled feet grind against gravel,
a sound like my mother's crying in the red chair.
The magnolia with its proud dark leaves,

yellow stamen bulb, and petals
drooping white envelopes of scent.
I'd feel small

except for the tiny crabapple next to it,
next to me, carrying tart cargo
everyone knows is the brains of this garden.

No one talks as much as the roses,
gossiping like the mean girls
making fun of my new bra.

Wind ruffles my hair with its fluster of kisses,
currents that bleed my heart raw.
I can almost smell

the faint diesel of the school bus,
but it's Sunday.
I look at the abandoned greenhouse

with its carcasses of orchids
alone in the hot quiet.
And sweet peas should be budding

but the arbor is leaning
like a fallen scarecrow
that's given up the field to the crows.

A jet weeps contrails overhead
on its way to someplace exotic,
someplace not here.

But here, in our mother's rose garden,
my arms around my thin white shoulders,
I imagine someone hugging me so tight

I can't breathe.

She said I shouldn't try
and tell you anything in a poem

so I won't. I won't tell you how I used to believe in angels sitting on the edge of my bed with its tight cornered sheets. Angels, perched there like quizzical birds waiting for instruction, a cocked head to the left as if to say "go on." My angels were tiny, troll sized, not even as big as Barbies and always interested in what I said and didn't say. It's odd really; we weren't from a religion that spoke of an afterlife. Maybe I'm making this up. Who would know? Lying is easy in a poem and what were they doing there, those angels? Were they protecting me? I don't think so. Too much happened in that room with the big windows and the view of the in-ground trampoline and the eucalyptus, and too much didn't happen. Like when I lost my virginity to a boy I barely knew, had just met. I wanted it to be dispensed with like a bank transaction that needed undoing, the returned check of my unloved body. Someone should have told me not to, that night with only the gray tabby as a witness and she was silent on the matter, probably already dying from the tumor I would discover too late to help her. And anyway, I'd met him at a party. He was there with my friend Jennifer and she sent him to take me home. He was hers and she gave him to me. Either she was trying to pawn him off or deliver me; I can't be sure. I shouldn't tell you how I lay coffin-stiff on that single bed while he did what he did and even after he left when I realized that nothing had changed except I was sore. I was still home for winter break. I was still lonely. I still hadn't sorted through the cupboard with its chorus of dolls I'd long outgrown.

In another life

I am not afraid of spiders or the soft
sticky dew-drenched web
touching my face in the yard.
Or perhaps, I am entirely coordinated,
a dancer, on point. My mother
has taken me to lessons
many times a week since I was three.
In another life, I have such a mother.
She remembers all the years
of ballet lessons. She comes
to every show and tells
all her bridge partners
about her famous daughter.

In another life my parents never die,
never get old or infirm. They teach me
how to grow a thriving garden.
I learn the name and care for
every rose. My dad plays baseball
with my son. My mother teaches
my daughter how to sew a ball gown.

In another life I am a bear,
foraging for voles and berries,
I know every corner of these woods
and I can recite each braid of silence
in every tongue but ours.

In this life, I am just a woman
who stops at the pond
where words swim like bright fish,
and takes a small sip there.
I'm a woman who speaks
to ghosts in her sleep,

who picks up the broken pieces
and tries hard to love them.

Where Do Poems Come From?

after Brendan Constantine

Sometimes in dreams,
or dangling from the tips of pine needles
like dew or tears.
A sickle moon perched in my chest
when I am alone and empty-headed.

I found my first under a still-warm sheet,
read another on his thigh
at the point of imprint with mine.

I found one on the beach
under that five-tunnel rock there in the sand
with all the sculpin and hermit crabs,
but the hole bloomed with water
before I could read it. I still have the rock.

In my vegetable garden once,
I collected October ghosts:
smashed remains of Sungolds, sharp spine
of artichoke flowers, one still-green Brandywine,
and there, with the delicate tomatillo skeletons,
was a poem. Unwritten, of course,
but like the green tomato,
I was sure it would ripen.

Sometimes a poem lies in wait
coiled and hissing. If it strikes,
I can suck the venom
from my thumb and hold a pen.

I'm certain there is a poem
that will answer all my questions
like a devoted mother

who—attentive to signs of distress—
carries her glassy-eyed child.
This poem carries the exact names of everything.
It knows my name,
not the one I was given, but the one
I was meant to have.

II

Or Am I Remembering It Wrong?

For All I Know

for my sister, Jan (1953-2012)

When I heard you were dead
I was looking at the blank space
in the front yard, the indent
in the lawn where the old white oak stood,
its ghost now shimmering
in the early spring light.
Even the dogwood misses that tree.
There was a swing when we moved in,
hanging from a sturdy branch twenty feet in the air.
I stood staring at the absence.

The last time we spoke, you said
your skin was totally white now,
the vitiligo you inherited from our mother
taking the last of the pigment.
You said your hair had gone white too,
when your daughter died.

When I heard you were dead,
I thought of the albino buffalo calf
born in North Texas—rare—one
in ten million, how he gave his people hope,
how later they found his mutilated body
left behind by people who hate.
I wondered what happened to his head,
that calf, how sometimes
even knowing you are endangered isn't enough.
I thought about your own daughter
dead by a needle last year.

I remember when you carved vines
down your arms with shards
of a broken mirror and left

the blood puddling on your floor
like some macabre red
midnight sea
reflecting the full moons
of our faces,
how we looked for
your body for an hour
and found only more blood.
That was thirty years ago.
You've been dying most of your life.

Just last month you called and said
you'd swallowed rat poison, neglecting
to say it had been weeks before.
The rat poison was organic and only
gave you a mild headache.
We kept you on the phone
until the ambulance came
and found you, this time in a puddle
of light, white haired, brow furrowed,
very much alive.

Tonight I imagine the shadows
of maple leaves on the pavement
outside your apartment. For all I know,
you died in your sleep.
For all I know, you never slept
through a single night.
For all I know, you never told me
the truth about anything.

I raise my right hand as if you are there
in my yard, by the new buds of Double Delights,
next to the white ghost of the white oak,
next to the white ghost of the white buffalo calf,
who nods his head once, and then lumbers away.

Oak

If my skin is ever slivered with bark
like the great white oak I lost in the front yard—

if I am ever wind-ravaged like that tree
and all my leaves desert me—

if the long ropes unravel, the ropes that carried the swing
where I sat and cried with my small crying child in my lap

when I had a small crying child and a rope swing
in a tree in the front yard—when I had a tree.

When I had a tree that didn't drop its heft,
an outstretched arm branch severed,

severed, that fell onto the roof screaming
I am broken. I am a wet and broken thing,

the way I screamed that time in the bathtub
in that tiny apartment on Purdue

before there were kids or houses or oak trees
and I screamed in the full-throated storm of grief,

skin curdling and pruny in that wet tempest.
in that apartment where I was a lost and broken thing

that needed your strong arms to fish me out
of that unmoored lake of sobbing.

If I am that broken thing ever again—
splintered bark, frayed rope, crater in the front yard—

if you find me like that again, curved in on myself,
chewing the wet grass, a spiral of skin and teeth and tears

dug deep in the hole where the white oak once stood,
cover me with moss and bark and leaves and feathers.

Make a bed there in the front yard.
Wrap your limbs around me.

Birthday

I buy you pink-tinged yellow roses on your birthday
because to me you are never gone; we take the elevator
to the cellar together, suffocate from the bad smells

at Walmart, a place you would never have gone;
you would worry that bad taste might be catching
like lice or bravado.

I know how you loved Opium,
not the drug, but the French perfume.
We went to the Côte D'Azur,
those cobblestone streets.
I can still hear the husk of your breath,
your low voice.

I want to ask you the names of trees
I should plant in my front yard
now that the oak with its muscular red leaves
is gone, now that I can see you from my bedroom,
growing there in that empty space
in the early light.

My Dead Mother Speaks to Me, Reminding Me She Is Not a Metaphor

Death is Rachmaninoff's 3ʳᵈ Concerto
played by Horowitz,
inflamed, and so loud
sparks fly from the white keys.

Death is also a black scorpion
in the desert,
tail curled
in anticipation.

The ocean is dismal with fog.
It comes in blankets that hover
but do not warm.
Fog is also death.

Even a tiny blond girl who jumps rope,
her ponytail leaping as she chants
in a voice that rattles like seeds
inside a gourd.

And the trampoline with broken springs,
buried in the ground
where rats play,
where cats find them.

I've been with Death all this time,
and still I am dizzy watching her hunt.
Death is sleek as any jaguar.
Her velvet coat shimmers, even at night.

But me, I am just a mom who remembers
when your hair was gold

and your eyes glimmered
while I read to you.

You always did exaggerate.
I am not Death. I am just dead,
and there is a difference.

Epithalamion on Highway Five
for Steve

So I unto my selfe alone will sing;
The woods shall to me answer and my Eccho ring.
　　　　　　　—Edmund Spenser, "Epithalamion"

Here I am in my car suddenly missing us,
the newborn us, on Third Avenue in Santa Cruz,
that basement apartment, the young us,
sitting on that couch for hours
reading Spenser's "Epithalamion" out loud,
that summer listening to Talking Heads on 8-track.
That apartment where I could see only
a person's feet when they approached.
That apartment with its damp smell
and tiny closed-in walls. You with so much
hair, me with such narrow hips. I was finishing
school and thinking about endings and beginnings,
but what was I beginning? Did we think we would stay
our twenty-year-old selves, unchanged and unfinished?

My first apartment alone but not really alone
because you were there, often, the too small bed
that wasn't really a bed, the sometimes lazy drip
of the sink if I didn't turn it just so, the two-burner stove.
I never understood how I could lose anything
in such a small room: my keys, an avocado,
my copy of Richard Lattimore's *Iliad*. I almost lost
you that summer. We both knew you'd be leaving.
Once I lost a huge spider I wanted you to evacuate.
I told you it looked like a shaggy mouse but you
never saw it. Like so much else in those days,
it disappeared but scared me anyway,
the way what's gone and can't be found
can be the most terrifying of all.

That was the summer you drove your Dodge Coronet
to visit your family. You sent funny postcards,
addressed to your nickname for me,
your driving adventures in Utah and Texas,
sleeping in your car. I didn't know if you'd ever
come back and you didn't know either.

Today I can see the wind jostling
the October-red leaves, and a bird,
an ordinary gray bird struggles to stay on course.
I see her blown sideways, flapping uselessly,
and I think, *Is this what's happened to us,*
is this how we got blown sideways into our sixties?
Not even a keepsake from that summer?

If I move aside the piles of bills and unfinished projects
to find my red copy of Spenser and let my tongue linger
on the words as if discovering them for the first time,
will you listen? Or am I remembering it wrong?

Elizabeth with Lettuces

Unblinking blue of water
from the park's view of Santa Monica Beach,
shimmering its ice next to the pier
with the pink and beige carousel,
I wheel you by the produce market,
up Arizona, past cactuses, flowers
and honey, while you are sleeping deep
amid throngs of people, tarragon and basil,
hanging ropes of garlic a dollar a head,
Chinese peas and sunflower sprouts,
past fruit stands (fruit is heavy, I'll do that last)
and vine-ripe warm tomatoes I cradle
next to the white eggplant I like
for its slick clean skin, forgoing
watermelon and strawberries,
I turn my attention to your sudden crying
ignoring the plums and peaches,
so I can pick you up and carry you,
yes, I am holding too much I say out loud,
I've loaded your stroller with bags
when a woman taps my shoulder
and hands me a crumpled five-dollar bill
fallen from my shirt pocket, and I push
vegetables aside to make room for you
and your feet crowded with red oak leaf,
dark arugula, zucchini the full length of your shin,
only the essentials, not like the purple irises
spilled when I retrieved you
from the car last week, and now,
where I wheel you back up the hill, stumble,
the bags, too many, into my trunk, slowly
I look at you, dressed in light olive
your pale skin glistening, the last to go,
the lettuces, everywhere, lettuce leaves

jammed around your tiny feet,
one red leaf between your toes,
kiss of radicchio climbing out of you, I pull
bits of sun green from your dark wavy hair,
and if I were a painter I'd paint you this way:
Elizabeth with Lettuces,
though you wouldn't stay still.

Stradivarius

As you walked under an open window,
a violin yielded itself to your hearing
  —Rainer Maria Rilke

My breath, held thin and delicate as a web
every time he falls off a chair, or the piano stool,
or the couch, every time he gets into my make-up
or the childproof medicine cabinet
or my heart, so many times a day.
He wants all of me, every fiber, every
sunlit inch of me. He wants my breasts
to suck and caress. I think he believes
they are part of his own body.
He wants my voice, which yells NO
and sings all his songs, reads his books.
He wants my hands to hold and walk and walk
and push the swing and get him out and get him back in and
push it some more and get him back out and walk some more
and get him crackers and rice cakes and water and more rice cakes.
My legs and feet and belly and neck and hair,
back and arms, my internal organs, my pulsating insides
for him. He wants to play me like a fine instrument
he can raise to his shoulder and render all other sounds
meaningless. He wants every mournful attenuation,
every elated staccato to be his. He wants
and wants and wants until finally he sleeps.
And I go in and watch him sleep so I can see him
not wanting me.

Heat

Summer bites sharp as shark's teeth, splash of cold on my watermelon red face & watermelon & marionberries & sweet caramel of bulbous boysenberries & the farmer's market twice yesterday after I forgot my lettuce with Pablo but remembered my berries & heat off cracked asphalt radiates radiates radiates & too hot for hugs & water the tomatoes three times a day & talk to them yes, sleep naked but the cat & her orange warm fur won't stay away & close the curtains like a shut in, don't turn the oven on god no god no god no & so many berries but too hot to make jam, all the boiling pots but leave bowls out cool water for the crows & squirrels & for hot humans cooling stations & in summer, grass the color of tan arms & fires, no no no fireworks & the chef who said someone measured the heat on his back & it was 150 degrees "like a good steak," he said & "that's too hot for a person" & my sister calls from a beach in Santa Barbara & sometimes she leaves messages on my machine "I miss him," she says of her husband who died of cancer, "it's so quiet here," but never when she's talking to me, only the machine bearing witness & now she tells me about her toes in the foam & the anemone bubbles & the sand & I can almost imagine my feet cool & wet & I tell her I read that someone drowns every 2 days & how everyone should be careful of riptides & how the calmest place, the darkest blue, the quietest is always the deadliest & why why why is that so often true.

Long After You're Gone

I cross the narrow field alone.
The starlight is a beacon
I follow all the way into morning.

Any day now I'll get through an hour
without missing you,
without that intense pang of wanting.

Almost a year now.
I can forgive you for dying
but not for still being dead.

One day, I might plant yellow tulips
in the hard and grieving winter earth,
submerge the small brown bulbs

as if they were quiet hearts beating.

Enough History

for Steve

Sometimes our life together is sprawling behind us
like a twisty ribbon of road through the hills.

Sometimes we're both in the car together.
Sometimes I see one of us on the side of the road
signaling for a pick up while the other drives on.
It's a small red convertible,
though we've never owned one.
Vintage, like we are. It's got a name that's sexier
than we've ever been: Spitfire or Bugatti.

Sometimes even in the tiny car together,
there are ghosts between us staring
like the creepy dolls in movies
that can't be killed, the eyes always open
even when ours flutter in the dark.

Or we forget to look at each other and only look
at the road ahead which always disappears
behind a sun-browned hill, before
I can see where it goes.

I'd say this was a sweet recipe
for growing old together,
one without the usual amount of sugar,
but it's always been this way with us,
meetings, partings, a softness in your voice at last
and your eyes finally here, waiting for me this time
after a long spell of distance.
The unseen surprises us every time,
the road unfurling as we drive.

I used to chase the car when I saw you
speed past without even noticing me
shouting your name. Now there is enough history
to know it won't be long before you remember.
And anyway, there's always a nice view
on the road while I wait.

Inflorescences

Once in a snowdrift of sleep
the sheet folded its crisp crease
like a heart looking in the cold for its twin.

I was not expecting anything.

Once in the hour between the storm
and my mother's dying voice,
I held my breath in the unlikeliest of dreams,
the absent syllables clustered
like marbles in my mouth.

Once where I live I gathered
evidence that I was loved:
the lingam the shape of an egg,
the Gilhoolie jar opener in the doodad drawer,
an overstuffed recipe box
with five different index cards
for cream of mushroom soup.

I gave my twenty-one-year-old daughter
Aladdin invitations I had bought
for her eight-year-old birthday party;
she was ecstatic.

Here in the cadence between pain's husky gasps,
the black wick sizzling like meat on the grill,
here in the hour between the scattering of salt
and the scattering of ashes, the departure

is a napkin left at the bar
folded into a white lily.
I was always alone
even when we were all here together.

The Dollhouse

Just when I think I've gotten used to loss
here they are again, the little doll family:
the mother, the father, the daughter,
the pet gerbil,

until the mother loses her footing
and falls down the stairs, until
the father pulls out a Colt and shoots himself,
until the daughter unleashes a blazing scream,
a pink-hair-yanked-out-by-the-roots scream.

On bad nights I see that my whole life happened
without my consent, the doll daughter
searching for her mother in the orchard.
She won't find her.
The garden is barren, empty of mothers.

Most of us know this story,
the story of the trapped family.
Sometimes they escape to the back yard.
Sometimes the dollhouse burns.
Sometimes the gerbil can be saved.

In Defense of Loneliness

You're wondering if I'm lonely
—Adrienne Rich

Are you asking about this moment
when the blue between clouds is so spare
I could be imagining it,
not imagining the blue
but the loneliness,
the space between what's missing
and what's there?

Not what's there, really,
but more the way birch bark separates
and peels like sunburned skin
and I can focus on the red burn,
how it turns white and prickles and blisters,
or the new bark underneath—
not bark but skin,
not new skin, but the pain
of what's left behind.

Sometimes I miss my mother's laugh
and I feel a cavern in the base of my belly,
not just my belly but everywhere
and it opens inside me
and then, yes, I think I am lonely.

So sometimes in the quiet emptiness
of early morning
when everyone's asleep,
I listen for their breathing,
then I listen for my own
and I am alone
but not lonely.

But what about that chasm
stretching before me sometimes,
not a cliff's edge really,
more like I'm an eagle whose talons
cannot be trusted to hold onto the branch,
not just any branch
but the most important branch.

Sometimes I miss my children
or my husband and they are sitting
two feet away and I am lonelier still.

And sometimes I would do anything
to speak in that shadow language:
fur and bone, wing and feather,
that tongue of peeling bark.
If we could all just listen
when the silence was unbearable.

Not quiet—which is different—
quiet which is full and open
and sometimes haunting.

If we could bear the silence though,
together, all of us,
that would be
something, wouldn't it?

Afterwards

All the hospital noises stopped
the buzzes and beeps
paging system
voices
footsteps

Even though we were crying
we made
no sound
Just after the breathing stopped
was the quietest moment

Dear Ghost

I shouldn't have been surprised, wasn't really
by the absence of you in this world, coming finally
after all the attempts to leave your mark
sometimes in red pools on the floor, or
red and blue blinking lights of the ambulance
in the driveway when I was nine
and quickly shoved into my room.

By the time you died, you were a stranger
not a sister, and I waited to hear the method:
heroin, pills, razor blades, even self-immolation
wouldn't have shocked me. I could almost smell
your burning pasty white skin.
What did surprise me was how you died,
the mystery of it, the lack of drama.
You had just been in the hospital,
the rabbi told my oldest sister, with pneumonia.
Perhaps they discharged you too soon,
we wondered out loud.

It's almost Mother's Day again. You,
gone a few days before, but years ago.
Your grown daughter had died.
Heroin overdose, the apple not falling far.
Still, yours was a quiet death, alone
in your apartment in Canada.
It's nearly the anniversary. It might be today.
None of us wrote it down.

Remember our house on Comstock Avenue?
Big windows overlooking the park,
the Chinese elm out in front

where a photographer captured
our pixie-cut childhood in black and white
before everything happened or didn't happen?

Dear Ghost, I was the silent starstruck one.
You glowed brighter than any of us.
How temporary incandescence can be.

III

I Don't Want to Miss It When It Finally Arrives

In Defense of Hallucination

Yesterday I saw Jimi Hendrix everywhere,
the top left corner of my bedroom window,
a ghost image behind me in a mirror,
a poster on the wall at the dentist's office
which usually just has a poster of a tooth.
A friend of my sister's once told me
she'd lost her virginity to Jimi Hendrix.
Is he a mirage in her bathroom mirror too?

If we imagine that we see the dead,
that we wander past them in dark hallways
and chase them in bright beads of water,
why not my sister in the shiny wreckage
of a broken martini glass,
my father in a fresh dusting of talcum powder?
Why not my mother under the Japanese magnolia
on the corner, that bursts with blooms one minute
and pink-litters the lawn the next?

Why can I see Jimi Hendrix and not my mother?
Like some *Where's Waldo*, I search for myself
in the Venetian tapestry of my life.
There is an urgent message I am supposed to receive.
I can feel it in the interstices of my bones.
I carry opera glasses and binoculars at all times.
I may even get a telescope.
I don't want to miss it when it finally arrives.

For Sale

The house was across from Holmby Park
and up a long driveway,
lavender wisteria climbing a trellis.
I remember that hot walk up the hill, I can see
the cottony seed masses of the floss silk tree,
feel the biting thorns of its trunk.

Yesterday I learned that the house was for sale.
I looked at the pictures over and over
like a potential buyer
with twelve million dollars lying around.
Just outside the pool is a rim of grass
where I burned my small feet on flagstone.
Later, we had the pool half-covered for my wedding.
Back then, my cluttered bedroom looked out
at the eucalyptus tree, the in-ground trampoline.
The new owners took all that out,
but my room is still there
minus the kittens in the closet.

My father died in that house, in the library.
I can imagine him studying the shelves that last night,
the built-ins covered in such a cacophony of titles,
Shakespeare, A. A. Milne, Michener, Galsworthy.
My mother looked out at the pool
where I learned to swim, the yard
sweet with sweet peas,
artichokes that bloomed to purple spikes,
roses and roses and roses.

A white-hot voltage sparks through my legs
when I look at those pictures.
The husk of my mother still lies
on the queen-sized bed

looking out at the palm trees,
their purple orchids grafted there,
the endlessly huge windows.
Even with eyes closed,
I could slide on stockinged feet
from my mother's bedroom, to the kitchen,
to my room to the little yard with various dogs.

The new owners mentioned an artist's studio
next to the garage.
So even with all the changes,
they kept that room
with its paint-spattered linoleum
where Dad created landscapes
that looked like hills on fire, and painted us.
I can still smell the oil.

When I Wasn't Looking

When I wasn't looking,
the wind beat against the bushes
outside Cabin #8
spattering the leaves like confetti,
knocking down the yellowjacket trap
and all its cargo.

While I was sleeping,
my son grew a beard.
The waves made a fierce reckoning sound,
a rhythmic crash and return
like words that can't be taken back.

When I wasn't paying attention,
the stephanotis spilled its fragrance
and dumped its tiny white trumpet flower
at the foot of a small blond girl.
Undone by that thick scent
she stopped mid jump.

I wish I hadn't missed that moon jellyfish
the size of my hand
slipping in and out of seaweed hair,
all its stomachs visible
to anyone who'd bother to look.

When I closed my eyes for just a second,
all the grandmothers sat around a table
in a smoke-filled dance hall,
each muttering to herself or maybe to me
but I wasn't there to hear the silver bangles
or smell the last ghost of Replique
as it wafted through the air.

When my back was turned,
a baby rolled over for the first time,
my daughter trembled like an oak leaf
just before falling.
She wept silently in her room.

The porch boards creaked from the weight
and warp of a winter storm,
a spider paused by the gold-green skeleton
of an abandoned tomatillo in my garden
before making its way
towards the wooden edge of the raised bed
and moving on.

What It Was Like to Lose My Mother

I believe I have a kind of feverish hunger
not a light flutter, more like the squall
we had in April, sudden.

And no, I do not define myself as orphan,
more like a blue iris in a swamp
where frogs sing loud as trumpets.

In the hazy dusk of that first afternoon,
I became ferocious, loss
a foreign country I had visited
against my will.

I heard a growl that began low and guttural,
traveled faster and faster.
People were afraid to come near me.
I was afraid to let them.

Colloquy
for Else

I speak to you in the car
even though you only drove for one day
in all eighty-nine years.

I speak to you in the car
and in the shower
a litany of unwashed words.

I speak to you in the car
when I drive by your apartment.
You're as far from me
as each drop of rain that you loved,
that you longed for, like I long for light,
for you.

I speak to you in the car. I tell you
I get it now, what it was like to want to be heard
when words were stuck in your mouth.

I speak to you in the car, in the dark, in the bathtub.
I tell you I remember when you put ice cubes
in the bathtub and soaked a beach towel,
put the wet freezing thing
on my burning five-year-old body.

No one can bring down my fever now.
My body is a white bridge
between worlds.

I speak to you in the car.
I yell this time.
"It's your turn to talk," I scream.

But we both know silence,
its grim portent,
how it weaves the dark into the dark.

She Wasn't Dripping Fudge
off a Wooden Spoon

Thirteen years ago today
my mom wasn't in her kitchen,
its red leather benches
so worn that the soft fuzz oozed
from where my sister's fingernails had scarred it.
Not in the kitchen with the window
looking out at the little yard
and a Newfoundland barking there.
Not standing at the white stove
stirring cream sauce for pasta
or burning bacon and not caring
because she loved it crisp.
She wasn't in the locked storage room
with the key we always hid
and she always found.
She wasn't looking for treasure:
sardines or anchovies in the pantry's dark cave.
And she wasn't dripping fudge off a wooden spoon
into a cup of cold water
to see if her fingers could coax it into a tight ball
so she would know that tiny offering
to the candy gods declaring: *enough*.
My mom wasn't licking Alfredo sauce
from stubby couldn't-reach-an-octave fingers.
She wasn't tending her cymbidiums
or arranging Double Delights
in a cut glass vase.
Thirteen years ago today her gravel voice
had dwindled to a rasp of drowning breath,
all of us crowded in that tiny room
around a hospital bed
as we had once crowded
around the mottled Formica

of the kitchen table.
As in the old days
we were all waiting for something
to be ready,
chicken in the pot,
peaches and raspberries,
matzos and eggs.
We were listening to Rachmaninoff's 3rd
and looking for a recipe
no one could find.

Heirloom Tomatoes

I come home from Orcas Island
inundated with smoke
from six hundred fires in Canada.

At home, the mole has made good work of the lawn;
its mounds are manifold. And the garden:
my 6 X 9 patch of dirt
cannot be contained by wood.
Tomatoes strain their cages.
The Brandywine has pulled over its house
like some recalcitrant child.

I find my Black Krims drooping,
neglected, some bulging and lumpy
like an old man's red face,
some soft, disappointed
it has taken so long to rescue them.

I come home from an island
where the last night
the sky finally cleared.
And the sunset melted all the way into the water.
By our canoe we saw seven otters swimming,
a brown eagle waiting in a tree.
Just a juvenile, no white head.

And here are my Sungolds waiting for me,
candy sweet, happy orange globes
saying, *It's okay. You're not too late.*

I study the mysterious Longkeepers,
new to my garden. I am told
they will last on the counter until February,
their green skins thick and sturdy.

Not all my tomatoes are heirlooms.
I look at the even round heads
of the Early Girls.
They too are part of the family.

I come home from the island
where two days after I left,
my friend, still there, sees four orcas
near her kayak, perhaps
at the moment I was talking
to my Green Zebras.

We both agreed
you can't be everywhere at once.

What I Tell Myself at 3 AM

Do I smell my mother's perfume
late at night and only in hallways
that have not been there before,
mute onyx statues lining the walls,
a red Chinese runner, my feet still cold,
dried roses lingering on my tongue?

I did not believe in wincing
when I reached into the open mouth
of a sea cave, the expanding
yaw of sand, not inviting to my fingers.
I don't believe in coincidence,
that there are five of us searching
the waters for a mother
to burrow into, tiny sand creatures
waiting. I do not believe it was a sign
when I pulled out a small gray rock
glistening and wet
with five random holes
for tiny creatures to hide.

I do not believe in signs
when the exhale of fog
forms a pattern in the dank
night soup, when the tea leaves meander
into a wolf's head and I hear the howl
and the echo. I do not believe in echoes
or studying my palm where the rock,
with a dazzle of hiding caves,
still waits for a scurrying daughter.

I do not believe in lost daughters
or mothers, waiting, seeing
my mother's form

in the persimmon tree,
each persimmon perfectly slick,
curved, almost carved,
the meat's soft squish in my mouth.
I do not believe my mother's ghost
lives in every garden that I love—
I do not believe in ghosts.

Double Sonnet in Memory of Elegance

My mother's long white evening gloves,
untouched in a drawer, waiting for hands
as a labyrinth waits for a minotaur.
Last night, outside, I admired the spider,
the symphony of its web, how any obstacle
can be navigated. Cosmetics
do not make you elegant.
The luster light gleams. I heard
there was a traveler mad with grief.
I sat and waited for him in the hotel lobby,
dressed only in contortions and taffeta.
I wanted all of it to mean something:
The Persian rug, the Miro on the wall,
the pianist and his violent up-thrusts of sound.

First, I merely had the notion of a word,
fragments of yesterday, longing,
every humming hair follicle.
I left at 4 AM.
My mother's ghost would meet me
only in that all-night coffee shop,
dyed blue carnations she wouldn't
have been caught dead with
while she lived. I was faint with laudanum,
the most elegant drug I could think of.
The French toast was luxuriating in syrup.
My mother, a red hibiscus in her hair.
The gloves glowed
in the glimmering fluorescents.

The Goodbye Train

Some days I can't believe it myself.
It's not how I imagined the world, up on the roof
looking out on the whole unblemished moon,
hearing her voice pulsing in my skull,

her unwashed hair flat against her head,
her head flat against the pillow,
my hand flat against her pale skin.

I have to go over it again and again
but whatever I did or didn't do,
the goodbye train keeps snorting along
murmuring in the insufferable light.
I feel so old without her.

"She's gone," I say
to the ophthalmologist, caseworker, pharmacist.

The goodbye train is gaining momentum.
I can't keep up. "Wait," I shout,
waving my arms, baton-like,
at the disappearing caboose.
"It's not how I imagined the world,"
I say out loud
and finish, "without her."

But there is nothing left in its wake
except a dull shimmering
and the vibration on the tracks.

"It Feels So Long Ago, Like It Wasn't Even Us"

for Steve

"I miss everything," you begin,
I remind you we are still alive.
I'm trying to find a way to answer
what you haven't asked,
like this whole life of one question after another.
"It's not like it was all perfect," you say,
and I think we'll go crazy from looking
for all the missing pieces,
like all the times you've lost your keys, even last week.

"Everything," you say, "645 Comstock.
That one time we had sex outside.
Where was that? No, not that time.
There were purple flowers.
My back got sunburned."

"Remember our first date?" I say,
"You made me red beans and rice
and I knew you were trying to impress me."
I don't say I miss you trying to impress me.

That basement apartment on Third Street,
how we read *The Faerie Queene* all night to each other
and didn't know that roots were growing between us.
We didn't know time had passed at all.

But I'm trying to get back to something I can picture:
"Pelicans!" I say. "We walked by a fence on a trail
and the kids were practically babies. *He* was in the backpack.
I had *her* by the hand and she still had curls."
I can't see your face but my hand is on your back
and your back remembers; I can tell this

just from the heat of it. There were so many pelicans
and we kept watching as they dove and dove for fish,
the exact shine of blue that day, the blindingness of it,
but neither of us can remember where the trail was.

"I miss that beach in Baja," you say, your leg
wrapped around my sore knee.
We still have so many sand dollars from that beach
where we did nothing days on end, nothing,
gorging on butter and $6.00 lobster,
on light, the us before kids, before
I waited all night for my mother to die,
before light itself was endangered.

I'm looking through the sweat and dust
of old photographs, the kind that never make it
into scrapbooks, the memories that swallow us
and spit us out like bad whiskey.
I'm trying to tell you about ghosts.

The warped wood under me, I think,
from that long swing that hung from the low branch
of the white oak. Holding the baby and swinging
and crying, both of us. And the splinters
I'd find later from that wood.

We are silent for a moment, breathing.

Then

after Cecilia Woloch

Didn't we stand there on West Cliff Drive
and listen to the love songs of sea lions?

And later, didn't I memorize
the smooth skin on your back,
the landscape I suddenly knew
I knew, scapular hills,
divot next to the hip bone?

And weren't we lost
before we even began,
the way the cave mouth opened,
the way we traced the path into each other?

You rescued me from the bathtub once,
womb-deep and shuddering.
Was I trying to drown?

You found me then, shipwrecked,
wrapped me in dry towels
until the shaking could end.
You kissed the sea from my lips,
hugged the chill away.

We were bright and new then, weren't we?
Glimmering even in dark waters,
the divine mist all around us?

And weren't the waves crashing that first night
and the sea lions barking?

The Goalkeeper

When someone kicks a ball
he leaps, thick gloved fingers
tip the ball up and over. Crisis averted.
White socks full of tiny black turf balls
litter my car, my house, his bed.
When he kicks, his foot goes straight out,
the ball vaults three-quarters of the field.
Because I am his mother, I know
the kick aches in his hip flexor.
Because I am the nautilus shell that hears him,
I hold my own hand to the thin muscle
on my body that hurts on his.
I remember the gray light
of his birth, the smell of his hair
when he nursed. I want to hold on tight
before the next leap and the next.

Your Body, Still Your Body

It's too good to last, this early sunshine in April,
this smell-of-cut-grass morning,
and this body, with its mirage of infinite breaths,
its lie of immortality.
Your body knows its own edges,
the hairs on your forearms,
how they bristle in the cold.
Your skin, how it loves and loses itself,
how it loves skin that isn't yours.
Your body knows cumin from turmeric.
It knows the splinter you remove with a needle
from the one that can get to your heart.
It knows the moment of constriction and stoppage.
Your body knows
breath, hearing, memory.
Your body knows sting and soothe,
the graffiti of cuts on your fingers,
the heat of a lover's hand on your back.
Your body knows how to stand stock still
and sequoia-strong and knows
it will not stand forever.
Your body knows there will be a time to leave,
a litany of lasts: last chocolate martini,
last walk on the beach, last walk
in the neighborhood, last purple bearded iris
and blooming dogwood,
last shell cupped
in the palm of the hand.
It knows how to savor lilac scent.
It knows this delight is temporary
as heartbeats. It knows
there is a finite number.
The body knows this even if

we get lost one night looking
at the halo around the moon
and forget.

Last Things

Tonight in the small hour,
I recite the last poem she read to me:
"Renascence," because today
would have been her birthday.

The last time I saw her,
her cheeks sucked in, mouth open,
we listened to Rachmaninoff's 3rd
all night, early sun through the hospital window.

The last trip we took together:
driving in Southern France,
a sip of Vermouth Cassis,
a twist of lemon, all felt forbidden at fifteen.
We sat in low chairs on a green lawn on a hill
looking out at other hills. Her yellow scarf,
wind-blown hair, her loud laugh
when I held the glass in timid hands.

When I was born, she didn't know I would live,
undone by the dumb luck of the order of things,
the placenta coming first.

I do this over again and again,
take stock of our lasts:
when we looked at orchids together,
when she was manic and didn't know me,
the last secret she kept from me,
last chaos, rushing to get there in time.

In the hospital, I stood
in the glaring fluorescents
holding her warm cracked hand
the last time I had a mother.

Before and After

Time stops if you stop long enough to hear it passing
—Rita Dove

Always a before
and an after.

The moment I forgot to know my father,
the moment after, when it was too late.

The moment before the phone call,
the waiting, when you know something

has happened,
but don't know what.

And now, all the long hot days this summer before,
finally, this week, rain.

Memory has its own unpredictable storms
and droughts. I can feel the air

in that long ago dining room
a silver bell, glass, chatter, before

a voice booms loud enough to echo,
to rattle the oil cityscape on the wall.

The clink of silverware then
silence, tears. Before. After.

If you listen hard enough
there is a hard stop just between.

A suspension, a held breath
a bridge.

Outside the dining room, the patio,
flagstone walkway, ferns,

a banana tree with no bananas.
My mother told me a woman coming in

from outside once walked right through
the clear glass dining room door

years before I was born.
Another before, another after.

If you really pay attention,
the silence before the shatter

is nearly deafening.

Water

That translucence astonishes me, and still,
when sunlight scatters its molecules
in the Caribbean, the sea appears blue,
in the Bahamas, aqua. Such a chameleon,
taking on the color of cliffs and dazzle.
I've seen the Sound murky and dark,
other times, a bright shimmer,
seen phytoplankton light its midnight depth
in a vein of green fire.

A still lake mirrors my face, water
remembering the stone that falls in it,
rings and rings and rings.
Tony Morrison said, "All water
has a perfect memory and is forever
trying to get back to where it was."
Like the rain today
drenching me and returning to itself,
the happy squish of feet in mud puddles,
the over and over again of water,
how it fills me and douses me,
splatters and surprises.

As a child I was invisible as water
poured clean in a glass.
When I learned to swim, in the final test,
I wore jeans and red sneakers.
Thrown into the pool, I hoped
to be welcomed there,
all my clothes wet and heavy, clinging,
as I made my body splash and rise,
reaching one hand for something solid.
Can water hold me? What can I hold?

I drink and drink, trying to return to myself.
I follow memory through its dark sea caves,
try to get back to where I was, swimming,
always upstream. The earth
is 71 percent water and still
so much of it hidden. I can be in water
and water in me. I can be at its edge.

I lie languid in a hot bath, lounging
in lavender-scented bubbles.
At night I dream of water, of losing my way,
waves overtaking me.
How much time have I spent looking at the sea?

When my mother was dying,
I listened to the gurgling,
her lungs, a babbling brook, then later
a tributary, a river not even
five of us could stop.
Finally, the ocean. Then, silence
so big, a mountain lake,
no movement anywhere.

Things I Never Knew I Loved
after Nazim Hikmet

I never knew I loved October
its light glint on leaves
the leaves themselves blushing and unsure

    I never knew I loved
the bite of morning air
and the scrambling of secrets
that live in mulch and loam in October

    and how much I loved sleep
until I couldn't sleep
the startled wake-up of pain
the ache trying to rest
against the cush of the pillow
    the dream that I loved too
gone now like a stallion galloping past
on young sturdy legs
when mine are neither

    and in the morning
the groggy eyes
luscious with sleep and I love it
so much I can't leave it

              even in October
when I never knew I loved garlic
    to eat it   yes
    but to hold the bulbous purple heads
    to ready the soil for seed
to feel the dry edges of the skin on my dry fingers
    the hopefulness of garlic
when the tomatoes are green
and unripening and finished with their seasons

because I knew I loved tomatoes
and now they're over like all those berries
which I knew I loved and the jam I made
and those glorious peaches
    but something
has to bring hope
when the fruit has died away
when the weeds have taken over
the promise of something still growing

           I don't always love hugs
but now that they are forbidden
I wish I could feel my friend's apricot scarf
touching my face when I hug her goodbye
    if only I could
    because now everything is off limits
except trees and how can I hug the trees
those very fine bits that prick into your skin
    almost invisible

          And even though I love manicures
I didn't know I loved dirt under my fingernails
    when I work the weeds out of the garlic bed
when the promise of something growing
seems all I can hope for
          I have always loved walking
the click of my sandals
on the street and the way wetness splashes up from the lawn
an almost imperceptible spray from grass to ankles

        But now that everything hurts
I think of my mother
her tired knees and hips making it difficult to move   but also how
she loved the smell of bacon cooking
    almost as much as the taste

I never knew I loved my mother's voice
until I couldn't hear it anymore
    heard instead
my own groans and clicks when I move my swollen knees
    now in October
    twenty years after her death
when I didn't know I'd love missing her

              imagining her here
as I imagine the stephanotis blossoms
    the lilacs
    all the exploding scents of spring
how what's gone lingers like someone's perfume

    In October
    when the sky is dimming
and it's too soon to plant the garlic
and the leaves are still holding
    desperately
    onto the branches

In the Quiet Place

I cannot hear the leaves fall
or the slipknot of oak bark,
the mist unveiling by the riverbed.
I can almost forget
the storm windows bolted shut,
the junkyard of blown glass,
the chill of the dream
where everything was ruined.

Both benches are alone
without passengers
facing away from the tree,
from each other,
the way we face away from the dead
but hear them.

Sometimes it's just a puff of words,
the squeaky hinge of a long-lost swing,
the temple of two benches,
clear and separate
in the swallowed light.
And you know
someone has lived here.

Notes

"What You Leave Behind"

Else Kristina Hansen (pronounced Elsa) came from
Denmark and lived with my family, helping to take care of us
when we were children. She was very much a second mother
to my brother, my sisters, and me. She died in 2013 after a
difficult period of expressive aphasia. Aebleskiver is a Danish
dessert, similar to donut holes, often made on New Year's
morning. Other Else poems in this book are "Long After
You're Gone" and "Colloquy."

"Where Poems Come From"

The title and inspiration come from Brendan Constantine's
poem "Where Do You Get Your Ideas?"

"Inflorescences"

Some plants produce a single flower on each flower stalk;
many, though, have flowers arranged in groups on the main
stalk. This is called an inflorescence. From *The Dorling
Kindersley Visual Dictionary* in slightly different wording.

The Shiva Lingam stone is a sacred stone in the Hindu
culture. They are collected at the banks of the Narmada River
once a year. The stones are naturally shaped like an egg.

"Then"

This poem was inspired by Cecelia Woloch's poem
"Anniversary."

"Your Body, Still Your Body"

The title is from the first line of the poem "a note on the body" by Danez Smith. I added the comma.

"Water"

Toni Morrison spoke the quote in "Water" in a talk at the New York Public Library in 1986.

"Things I Never Knew I Loved"

The title and inspiration come from Turkish poet, Nazim Hikmet's poem "Things I Didn't Know I Loved."

"In the Quiet Place"

This poem was written after a photograph by Russell Young and appears in a wonderful book of photographs and poems, entitled *In the Mist*.

Acknowledgements

The following poems have appeared in journals, anthologies, or books, sometimes in slightly different forms.

Calyx Journal: "Your Body, Still Your Body," winner of the 2020 Lois Cranston Prize.

Catamaran Literary Reader: "Water."

Chance of a Ghost (Anthology): "What I Tell Myself at 3 AM."

Cider Press Review: "At the Mahogany Table."

Cloudbank: "Where Do Poems Come From."

In the Mist (photography book): "In the Quiet Place."

Fireweed: "Double Sonnet in Memory of Elegance."

Live Encounters Poetry: "In Another Life," "The Dollhouse," "The Goodbye Train," and "Repast."

The Poeming Pigeon: "The Goalkeeper."

Prairie Schooner: "Inflorescences," "What It Was Like to Lose My Mother," (published as "What It Was Like").

The Ravens Perch: "At Fourteen," "What You Leave Behind," "Last Things," and "Enough History."

Talus and Scree: "Elizabeth with Lettuces."

US1 Worksheets: "Nomenclature," "The Photograph," "Colloquy," "In the Quiet Place," and "Then."

Verseweavers: "For All I Know" Fall, 2013 1st prize in Poet's Choice award. "In Defense of Loneliness" Fall, 2017 2nd prize in Poet's Choice Award.

VoiceCatcher Journal: "White Lies."

Windfall: "When I Wasn't Looking," "Heirloom Tomatoes."

Personal Acknowledgements

There are many people to thank.

For her close reading of each poem and invaluable help in ordering the manuscript, I am indebted to Andrea Hollander.

For reading the entire manuscript and through her brilliant "riffing" finding the exact right title, much gratitude goes to Paulann Petersen.

I am so lucky to have Cathy Colman who has been my poetry sister longer than anyone. She has given me meaningful feedback on individual poems and the manuscript as a whole.

With gratitude to the amazing poets from my critique and prompt groups. Thanks to Margaret Chula, Christine Delea, Cindy Gutiérrez, Diane Holland, Andrea Hollander, Judith Montgomery, Paulann Petersen, Joanna Rose, Penelope Scambly Schott, Suzanne Sigafoos, and Dianne Stepp for their comments on some of these poems.

I want to thank members of my family of origin for their support and for living through much of this history with me: Mark Prinzmetal, Rachael Jayne, and Karen Prinzmetal.

For everything, thank you Steve, Elizabeth, and Daniel. Your love has sustained and nurtured me. I also appreciate your tolerance in finding yourselves in some of these poems.

Much gratitude to Lana Hechtman Ayers, editor and publisher of MoonPath Press, for selecting this manuscript for publication and for guiding me to find the book it was meant to be.

About the Author

Donna Prinzmetal is a poet and psychotherapist living in Portland, Oregon. She is the recipient of the 2020 Lois Cranston Prize from *Calyx*. Her first book, *Snow White, When No One Was Looking*, was published with CW Books in May of 2014. *Each Unkept Secret*, a finalist for the Concrete Wolf Albiso Award, is her second book.